FOOD LOVERS

CUPCAKES AND BAKES

FOOD LOVERS

CUPCAKES AND BAKES

RECIPES SELECTED BY JONNIE LÉGER

Trans
Atlantic
Press

For best results when cooking the recipes in this book, buy fresh ingredients and follow the instructions carefully. Note that as a general rule vulnerable groups such as the very young, elderly people, pregnant women, convalescents and anyone suffering from an illness should avoid dishes that contain raw or lightly cooked eggs.

For all recipes, quantities are given in standard U.S. cups and imperial measures, followed by the metric equivalent. Follow one set or the other, but not a mixture of both because conversions may not be exact. Standard spoon and cup measurements are level and are based on the following:

1 tsp = 5 ml, 1 tbsp = 15 ml, 1 cup = 250 ml / 8 fl oz.

Note that Australian standard tablespoons are 20 ml, so Australian readers should use 3 tsp in place of 1 tbsp when measuring small quantities.

The electric oven temperatures in this book are given for conventional ovens with top and bottom heat. When using a fan oven, the temperature should be decreased by about 20–40°F / 10–20°C – check the oven manufacturer's instruction book for further guidance. The cooking times given should be used as an approximate guideline only.

CONTENTS

STRAWBERRY CUPCAKES	6
CHOCOLATE GANACHE TARTS	8
TOFFEE CUPCAKES	10
ORANGE MUFFINS	12
CHOCOLATE APPLE MUFFINS	14
PEANUT MUFFINS with CRISPY TOPPING	16
BANANA and WALNUT MUFFINS	18
ICED CUPCAKES	20
BLACKBERRY MUFFINS	22
COCONUT CUPCAKES	24
ESPRESSO CUPCAKES with MASCARPONE CREAM	26
VANILLA CUPCAKES with BUTTERCREAM FROSTING	28
LEMON MERINGUE CUPCAKES	30
COFFEE and PECAN CUPCAKES	32
CHOCOLATE CHERRY CAKES	34
ORANGE and ALMOND MUFFINS	36
CUPCAKES with ICE CREAM LAYERS	38
CUPCAKES with ORANGE FILLING and CHOCOLATE SAUCE	40
MINI MUFFINS with ALMONDS	42
CHOCOLATE MUFFIN with CREAM FILLING	44
REDCURRANT and BLUEBERRY MUFFINS	46
BEE STING CUPCAKES	48
APRICOT and GINGER MUFFINS	50
CHRISTMAS CUPCAKES	52
APPLE MUFFINS with CARAMEL	54
BUTTERFLY BUNS	56
APPLE CAKES	58
MINI CHERRY MUFFINS	60
CHOCOLATE MUFFINS with ORANGE CREAM	62
BERRY CUPCAKES	64
FAIRY CAKES with JAM FILLING	66
ICED CHOCOLATE CUPCAKES	68
RASPBERRY and COCONUT MUFFINS	70
CHOCOLATE MUFFINS with FONDANT FILLING	72
RASPBERRY MUFFINS with VANILLA CREAM	74
HAZELNUT and CHOCOLATE CUPCAKES	76
BLACKBERRY and RASPBERRY MUFFINS	78
HUMMINGBIRD CAKES	80
GINGERBREAD BUNS	82
ANGELFOOD CUPCAKES	84
CHOCOLATE and BANANA MUFFINS	86
CINNAMON and MACADAMIA MUFFINS	88
CARROT MUFFINS with WALNUTS	90
LEMON CUPCAKES	92
CHOCOLATE CHIP MUFFINS	94

STRAWBERRY CUPCAKES

Ingredients

For the strawberry mousse:

8 oz / 250 g sliced fresh strawberries

1-2 tbsp sugar

5 oz / 150 g mini marshmallows

1 scant cup / 200 ml whipping cream

For the cupcakes:

2 eggs

Heaped ½ cup / 110 g superfine (caster) sugar

Scant ¼ cup / 50 ml whipping cream

1 tsp vanilla extract

1 cup / 110 g self-rising flour

½ tsp baking powder

4 tbsp / 50 g butter, melted

Confectioners' (icing) sugar, to decorate

Method

Prep and cook time: 1 hour plus 2 hours chilling time

1 For the strawberry mousse: Put the strawberries into a pan with a scant ½ cup / 100ml water and the sugar. Bring to a boil and simmer for about 3 minutes until the strawberries are soft. Remove from the heat and mash until pulpy.

2 Stir the marshmallows into the hot pulp until they dissolve. Leave to cool.

3 Whip the cream until it holds its shape but is not stiff. Fold the cream into the cooled strawberry mixture, then spoon into a bowl and chill for about 2 hours until set.

4 Heat the oven to 350ºF (180ºC / Gas Mark 4). Grease a 10-hole bun tin.

5 For the cupcakes: Beat the eggs and sugar until combined, then beat in the cream and vanilla.

6 Sift over the flour and baking powder and fold in lightly, followed by the butter.

7 Three-quarters fill the bun tins with the mixture. Bake for 12–15 minutes until golden. Test by lightly pressing the top of the cakes with your fingers – the cake should spring back.

8 Remove from the oven and leave to cool in the tins for 5 minutes. Turn out onto a wire rack to cool.

9 Split each cold cupcake into three, using a sharp knife. Place a spoonful of the mousse on one layer and spread fairly thickly over the cake. Top with a layer of cupcake. Spread with another spoonful of mousse and top with the third layer of cake.

10 Chill until ready to serve. Sift a little confectioners' sugar over the top layer just before serving.

Makes 10

CHOCOLATE GANACHE TARTS

Ingredients

1½ cups / 150 g all-purpose (plain) flour

1 tbsp cornstarch (cornflour)

¼ cup / 50 g superfine (caster) sugar

7 tbsp / 100 g butter, chopped

For the ganache:

¾ cup / 175 ml whipping cream

6 oz / 175 g bittersweet (plain) chocolate (70% cocoa solids), chopped

2 tbsp / 25 g butter

For the filling:

Cake crumbs

2–3 tbsp orange juice

Method
Prep and cook time: 45 min

1 To make the dough, put the flour, cornstarch (cornflour), sugar, and butter in a large bowl and mix together by hand until the dough sticks together. Add a splash of water if it is too dry. Chill the dough in the refrigerator for 30 minutes.

2 Preheat the oven to 375°F (190°C / Gas Mark 5). Grease a 12-hole muffin pan.

3 Divide the dough into 12 equal-size balls. Place one ball in each muffin cup and press down and around the sides to form a hollow shell.

4 Bake in the oven for about 15–20 minutes until golden, pricking the bases with a fork every 3 minutes to stop the dough from rising. Transfer to a wire rack and leave to cool.

5 Meanwhile, make the ganache. Bring the cream to the boil in a saucepan. Remove from the heat and stir in the chocolate until melted. Add the butter, stirring until the mixture is glossy. Leave to cool and then chill in the refrigerator until thick.

6 Mix the cake crumbs with the orange juice. Divide the soaked crumb mixture evenly between the cold tart shells.

7 Whisk the ganache with an electric whisk until increased in volume and thick. Spoon the ganache into a piping bag and pipe on top of the crumbs.

Makes 12

TOFFEE CUPCAKES

Ingredients

2¼ cups / 225 g all-purpose (plain) flour

Scant ½ cup / 90 g superfine (caster) sugar

2 tsp baking powder

Pinch of salt

1 egg, beaten

²/3 cup / 150 ml milk

¼ cup / 50 ml sunflower oil

1 tsp vanilla extract

For the toffee cream:

Heaped ½ cup / 115 g sugar

2 tbsp water

Pinch of salt

1¾ cups / 400 ml whipping cream

For the caramel sauce:

1¼ cups / 250 g superfine (caster) sugar

4 tbsp water

²/3 cup / 150 ml whipping cream

4 tbsp / 50 g butter

Method

Prep and cook time: 40 min plus 40 min chilling time

1 Preheat the oven to 400°F (200°C / Gas Mark 6). Line a 12-hole muffin pan with paper muffin cases.

2 Sift the flour, sugar, baking powder and salt into a large bowl.

3 Put the egg, milk, oil and vanilla extract in a jug and whisk together with a fork. Stir into the dry ingredients until combined. Spoon the mixture equally into the muffin cases.

4 Bake in the oven for about 20 minutes until golden brown and risen. Leave in the pan for 5 minutes and then transfer to a wire rack and leave to cool.

5 Meanwhile, make the toffee cream. Put the sugar, water and salt in a saucepan and cook over a medium heat, stirring once, until sugar has dissolved. Continue cooking, but do not stir, until sugar turns golden amber. Remove from the heat.

6 Slowly pour the cream into the pan, taking care as it will spatter. Heat gently, stirring until combined. Pour the caramel cream into a large bowl and leave to cool. Chill in the refrigerator for about 40 minutes until cold, stirring occasionally.

7 To make the caramel sauce, put the sugar into a heavy-based skillet (frying pan) and stir in the water. Heat gently, tilting the pan, until the sugar has dissolved. Do not stir or the sugar will crystallize. Increase the heat and bubble for 4–5 minutes until golden brown. Remove from the heat and carefully stir in the cream and butter. Pour into a jug or bowl and leave to cool.

8 To serve, whisk the toffee cream until soft peaks form. Spoon into a piping bag and pipe on top of the cold cupcakes. Drizzle with caramel sauce and serve immediately.

Makes 12

ORANGE MUFFINS

Ingredients

For the muffins:

5 tbsp / 75 g butter, melted

1 egg, lightly beaten

¾ cup / 175 ml plain yogurt

Juice and finely grated zest of
1 large orange

Juice ½ lemon

2½ cups / 250 g all-purpose
(plain) flour

1 tbsp baking powder

¾ cup / 150 g sugar

1 tbsp orange marmalade

For the glaze:

Juice and finely grated zest of
1 large orange

6 tbsp confectioners' (icing) sugar

2 tsp orange marmalade

Method

Prep and cook time: 40 min

1 Heat the oven to 375°F (180°C / Gas Mark 5).
Arrange paper baking cups in a 10-hole muffin pan.

2. Combine the butter, egg, yogurt, orange juice and
zest and lemon juice in a mixing bowl. Stir in the
flour, baking powder and sugar. Gently stir in the
marmalade.

3 Spoon the mixture into the paper cases, almost to
the top. Bake for 25 minutes until golden and risen.
Leave to stand for 5 minutes, then place on a wire
rack to cool.

4 For the glaze, beat all the ingredients together in
a bowl. The mixture should be thick enough to coat
the back of a spoon, but still fluid.

5 Spoon the glaze over the muffins.

Makes 10

CHOCOLATE APPLE MUFFINS

Ingredients

2¾ cups / 275 g all-purpose (plain) flour

4 tbsp cocoa powder

Heaped 1 cup / 225 g light brown sugar

1 tbsp baking powder

¼ cup / 50 ml sunflower oil

4 tbsp / 50 g butter, melted

2 eggs

¾ cup / 175 ml milk

1 cooking apple, peeled, cored and diced

For the decoration:

2½ oz / 75 g white chocolate (20% cocoa butter), coarsely grated

Method

Prep and cook time: 35 min

1 Heat the oven to 350ºF (180ºC / Gas Mark 4). Grease 12 muffin tins.

2 Sift the flour, cocoa, sugar and baking powder into a mixing bowl.

3 Beat the oil and butter with the eggs and milk until combined. Stir lightly into the dry ingredients but don't over-mix; the mixture should be slightly lumpy. Fold in the apples.

4 Spoon into the muffin tins until three-quarters full.

5 Bake for 20–25 minutes until risen and golden and a skewer inserted into the middle comes out clean. Cool in the tins for 5 minutes then place on a wire rack to cool.

6 Scatter the grated white chocolate over the top of the muffins.

Makes 12

PEANUT MUFFINS WITH CRISPY TOPPING

Ingredients

2¾ cups / 275 g all–purpose (plain) flour

Generous ¾ cup / 175 g sugar

1 tablespoon baking powder

Pinch of salt

2 eggs

¾ cup / 175 ml milk

¼ cup / 50 ml sunflower oil

4 tbsp / 50 g butter melted

4 oz / 110 g smooth peanut butter

For the peanut buttercream:

5 oz / 150 g smooth peanut butter

1 stick / 115 g butter

¾ cup / 90 g confectioners' (icing) sugar

For the crispy peanut topping:

1 cup / 200 g sugar

175 g / 1¼ cups unsalted peanuts lightly crushed

Method

Prep and cook time: 50 min

1 Heat the oven to 350ºF (180ºC / Gas Mark 4). Place paper cases in a 12-hole muffin tin. Line a cookie sheet (baking tray) with non-stick baking paper.

2 Sift the flour, sugar, baking powder and salt into a mixing bowl.

3 Beat the eggs, milk, oil, butter and peanut butter together until combined and stir in to the dry ingredients until just mixed. The mixture should be slightly lumpy.

4 Spoon into the paper cases and bake for 20–25 minutes until golden and risen. Cool in the tin for 5 minutes, then place on a wire rack to cool.

5 For the peanut buttercream, whisk the peanut butter and butter with an electric whisk until smooth. Add the sugar and whisk until fluffy.

6 For the crispy peanut topping, heat the sugar in a pan until melted and golden brown. Do not stir. Remove from the heat and add the peanuts, stirring well. Pour onto the lined cookie sheet (baking tray) and leave to cool and set for a few minutes, then break up into pieces.

7 Spoon the peanut butter cream into a piping bag and pipe on top of the muffins. Decorate with the crispy peanut pieces.

Makes 12

BANANA AND WALNUT MUFFINS

Ingredients

5 tbsp / 75 g butter

2½ cups / 250 g self-rising (self-raising) flour

1 tsp baking powder

½ teaspoon baking soda (bicarbonate of soda)

Pinch of salt

Heaped ½ cup / 115 g superfine (caster) sugar

2 eggs

1 tsp vanilla extract

½ cup / 125 ml milk

2 large ripe bananas

4 oz / 115 g chopped walnuts

To decorate:

4 tbsp crème fraîche or plain yogurt

4 tbsp runny honey

Method

Prep and cook time: 35 min

1 Preheat the oven to 375°F (190°C / Gas Mark 5). Line a 12-hole muffin pan with paper muffin cases.

2 Melt the butter. Sift the flour, baking powder, baking soda (bicarbonate of soda) and salt into a large bowl. Stir in the sugar.

3 Put the eggs, vanilla extract, milk and melted butter in a jug and beat together with a fork until combined.

4 Put the bananas in a bowl and mash well with a fork. Stir into the egg mixture.

5 Make a well in the center of the dry ingredients and add the egg mixture with the walnuts, stirring roughly with a fork (don't over-mix) until it is a lumpy paste. Spoon the mixture equally into the muffin cases.

6 Bake in the oven for 20-25 minutes until golden brown, risen and springy to the touch. Leave in the pan for 5 minutes and then transfer to a wire rack and leave to cool.

7 Place a spoonful of crème fraîche or yogurt on top of each muffin and drizzle with a little honey to decorate before serving.

Makes 12

ICED CUPCAKES

Ingredients

1 stick / 115 g butter

½–⅔ cup / 120 g superfine (caster) sugar

2 eggs, beaten

Heaped 1 cup / 120 g self-rising flour

½ tsp baking powder

1 tsp vanilla extract

For the frosting:

1¼ cup / 170 g confectioners' (icing) sugar

2 tbsp lemon juice

1 tsp hot water

Few drops pink food coloring

Pink and white sprinkles, to decorate

Method

Prep and cook time: 30 min

1 Preheat the oven to 350°F (180°C / Gas Mark 4). Line a 12-hole muffin pan with paper cases.

2 Put the butter and sugar in a large bowl and, using an electric whisk, beat together until light and fluffy.

3 Add the eggs gradually, beating well after each addition. Sift in the flour and baking powder and gently fold into the mixture. Stir in the vanilla extract. Spoon the mixture equally into the paper cases.

4 Bake in the oven for 12–15 minutes until springy to the touch. Transfer to a wire rack and leave to cool.

5 When cold, make the frosting. Sift the confectioners' (icing) sugar into a large bowl and gradually stir in the lemon juice and water until smooth.

6 Put half the frosting in another bowl and add a few drops of pink food coloring.

7 Spoon a little frosting on each cupcake and smooth the surface with a palette knife. Decorate with pink and white sprinkles and leave to set.

Makes 12

BLACKBERRY MUFFINS

Ingredients

1 stick / 110 g butter

1/3 cup / 75 g white sugar

2 tbsp dark brown sugar

2 eggs

1½ cups / 175 g all-purpose
(plain) flour

1 tbsp baking powder

2 tsp vanilla extract

Scant ¼ cup / 50 ml apple juice

¼ cup / 60 ml water

3 oz / 75 g blackberries

For the blackberry compote:

¼ cup / 50 ml blackberry liqueur

¼ cup / 50 g sugar

2 cups / 250 g blackberries

Method

Prep and cook time: 45min

1 Heat the oven to 375ºF (190ºC / Gas Mark 5).
Place paper cases in a 10-hole muffin tin.

2 Cream the butter until light then beat in the white
sugar and dark brown sugar until fluffy.

3 Add the eggs, beating well until combined.

4 Sift in the flour and baking powder and fold
into the mixture, followed by the vanilla extract,
apple juice, water and blackberries.

5 Spoon into the paper cases. Bake for 25 minutes
until golden and risen. Leave in the tins for
5 minutes then place on a wire rack to cool.

6 For the blackberry compote, heat the sugar and
liqueur in a pan and simmer for 2 minutes.

7 Add the blackberries and simmer for a further
2–3 minutes, or until the blackberries are tender
and the mixture has just thickened.

8 Place the muffins on serving plates. Spoon a little
blackberry compote alongside each muffin.

COCONUT CUPCAKES

Ingredients

1½ sticks / 175 g butter, softened

Heaped 1 cup / 225 g superfine
caster) sugar

2 eggs

1 tsp vanilla extract

2¼ cups / 225 g all-purpose
(plain) flour

2 tsp baking powder

½ cup / 125 ml plain yogurt

6 oz / 175 g sweetened flaked coconut
plus extra to decorate

For the frosting:

1½ cups / 175 g confectioners'
(icing) sugar

2 tbsp lemon juice

1 tsp hot water

Method

Prep and cook time: 45 min

1 Preheat the oven to 350°F (180°C/Gas Mark 4).
Line a 12-hole muffin pan with paper muffin cases.

2 Put the butter and sugar in a large bowl and,
using an electric whisk, beat together until light and
fluffy. Beat in the eggs and vanilla extract.

3 Sift in the flour and baking powder and gently
fold into the mixture with the yogurt, until well
combined. Stir in the coconut. Spoon the mixture
equally into the muffin cases.

4 Bake in the oven for 25-30 minutes until golden
brown and springy to the touch. Leave in the pan for
5 minutes and then transfer to a wire rack and leave
to cool.

5 When the cupcakes are cold, make the frosting.
Sift the confectioners' (icing) sugar into a bowl and
gradually stir in the lemon juice and water until
smooth.

6 Spoon a little frosting on top of each cupcake and
smooth the surface with a palette knife. Sprinkle
with sweetened flaked coconut and leave to set
before serving.

Makes 12

ESPRESSO CUPCAKES WITH MASCARPONE CREAM

Ingredients

5 tbsp / 75 g butter

2½ cups / 250 g all-purpose (plain) flour

2 tsp baking powder

¼ cup / 50 g light brown sugar

1 egg, beaten

7 tbsp cold strong black coffee

3 tbsp buttermilk

For the mascarpone cream:

1½ sticks / 175 g butter, softened

2¾ cups / 350 g confectioners' (icing) sugar

1 cup / 225 g mascarpone

2 tsp cold strong black coffee

Ground cinnamon for dusting

Method

Prep and cook time: 40 min

1 Preheat the oven to 350°F (180°C / Gas Mark 4). Line a 12-hole muffin pan with paper cases.

2 Melt the butter. Sift the flour and baking powder into a large bowl. Stir in the sugar.

3 Stir the egg and melted butter together and then stir in the coffee and buttermilk. Gently stir into the dry ingredients until just combined. Spoon the mixture equally into the paper cases.

4 Bake in the oven for about 25 minutes until risen and springy to the touch. Leave in the pan for 5 minutes and then place on a wire rack to cool.

5 To make the mascarpone cream, beat the butter in a large bowl until soft and then sift in the sugar. Gradually add the mascarpone until smooth and creamy. Stir in the coffee.

6 Spoon a little mascarpone cream on top of each cupcake and sprinkle with ground cinnamon to decorate before serving.

Makes 12

VANILLA CUPCAKES WITH BUTTERCREAM FROSTING

Ingredients

1½ sticks / 175 g butter

¾–1 cup / 175 g sugar

1 tsp vanilla extract

4 eggs, beaten

1½ cups / 175 g self-rising flour

For the buttercream:

5 tbsp / 75 g butter

1⅓ cups / 175 g confectioners' (icing) sugar

Few drops vanilla extract

To decorate:

12 raspberries

Method

Prep and cook time: 35 min

1 Heat the oven to 350ºF (180ºC / Gas Mark 4). Place paper cases in a 12-hole bun tin.

2 Cream the butter and sugar in a mixing bowl until light and fluffy.

3 Stir in the vanilla. Gradually beat in the eggs, beating well.

4 Sift in the flour and gently fold into the mixture until combined.

5 Spoon into the paper cases and bake for 20 minutes until golden and risen.

6 Leave in the tins for 5 minutes. Place on a wire rack to cool.

7 For the buttercream, beat the butter in a bowl until soft.

8 Sift in the confectioners' sugar and beat well. Stir in the vanilla.

9 Spoon into a piping bag. Pipe a whirl onto each cake. Top with a raspberry.

Makes 12

LEMON MERINGUE CUPCAKES

Ingredients

1 stick / 115 g butter, softened

Heaped ½ cup / 115 g superfine (caster) sugar

2 eggs

Heaped 1 cup / 115 g self-rising flour

Grated zest 1 lemon

1 lemon, to decorate

For the meringue:

2 egg whites

Heaped ½ cup / 115 g superfine (caster) sugar

Method

Prep and cook time: 35 min

1 Preheat the oven to 350°F (180°C/Gas Mark 4). Line a 12-hole muffin pan with paper muffin cases.

2 Put the butter and sugar in a large bowl and, using an electric whisk, beat together until light and fluffy.

3 Add the eggs, one at a time, and beat until fully incorporated into the mixture.

4 Fold in the flour and lemon zest until well combined. Spoon the mixture equally into the muffin cases.

5 Bake in the oven for 15–20 minutes, until golden brown and springy to the touch.

6 Meanwhile, make the meringue. Whisk the egg whites until soft peaks form. Gradually add the sugar, whisking continuously, until stiff peaks form and the mixture is thick and glossy.

7 Heat the grill to its highest setting.

8 Spoon the meringue over the cupcakes and form into spikes using a knife.

9 Place the cupcakes under the hot grill for 2-3 minutes, or until the meringue is tinged golden-brown.

10 Using a vegetable peeler, pare thin curls of lemon zest from the lemon and scatter over the meringue.

Makes 12

COFFEE AND PECAN CUPCAKES

Ingredients

1½ cups / 175 g self-rising flour

1½ sticks / 175 g butter, softened

Heaped ¾ cup / 175 g superfine (caster) sugar

3 eggs

3 tbsp cold espresso coffee

¾ cup / 75 g chopped pecan nuts

For the coffee butter cream:

1 stick / 115 g butter, softened

1⅓ cups / 200 g confectioners' (icing) sugar

3 tbsp cold espresso coffee

To decorate:

12 pecan halves

Method

Prep and cook time: 25 min

1 Preheat the oven to 350°F (180°C / Gas Mark 4). Line a 12-hole muffin pan with paper cases.

2 Put the flour, butter, sugar and eggs in a large bowl and beat together until well combined using an electric whisk.

3 Stir in the coffee and pecans. Divide the mixture equally between the paper cases.

4 Bake in the oven for about 15 minutes until risen and firm to the touch. Transfer to a wire rack and leave to cool.

5 To make the coffee butter cream, put the butter in a large bowl and beat until soft. Sift in the confectioners' (icing) sugar and beat well until pale and light. Add the coffee and mix well together.

6 Spread the coffee butter cream over the top of each cupcake and press a pecan half on top to decorate.

Makes 12

CHOCOLATE CHERRY CAKES

Ingredients

3 oz / 75 g milk chocolate (25% cocoa solids), chopped

1 stick / 115 g butter

1 cup / 200 g superfine (caster) sugar

1 egg, beaten

1 cup / 250 ml buttermilk

1 tsp vanilla extract

2½ heaped cups / 275 g all-purpose (plain) flour

1 tsp baking soda (bicarbonate of soda)

12 fresh cherries with stems

Method

Prep and cook time: 35 min

1 Preheat the oven to 375°F (190°C / Gas Mark 5). Line a 12-hole muffin pan with paper muffin cases.

2 Break the chocolate into a heatproof bowl and add the butter. Microwave on High for 1 minute or until softened. Stir and microwave for a further 15 seconds until melted. Alternatively, melt in a bowl standing over a saucepan of gently simmering water. Remove from the heat and stir until smooth. Leave to cool slightly.

3 Put the sugar, egg, buttermilk and vanilla extract in a large bowl and mix together. Stir in the melted chocolate.

4 Sift in the flour and baking soda (bicarbonate of soda) and gently stir into the mixture until combined.

5 Spoon the mixture equally into the muffin cases. Place a cherry into the center of each cake.

6 Bake in the oven for about 25 minutes until the cakes are springy to the touch. Leave in the pan for 5 minutes and then transfer to a wire rack and leave to cool.

Makes 12

ORANGE AND ALMOND MUFFINS

Ingredients

2 cups / 200 g all-purpose (plain) flour

1 tablespoon baking powder

Generous 1 cup / 225 g sugar

2/3 cup / 75 g ground almonds

2 eggs

1 stick / 110 g butter, melted

3/4 cup / 175 ml milk

3 tablespoons chopped
blanched almonds

Finely grated zest of 1 orange

For the orange buttercream:

10 tbsp / 140 g butter

2 cups / 250 g confectioners'
(icing) sugar

Juice and finely grated zest of 1 orange

To decorate:

Chocolate sprinkles

Method

Prep and cook time: 45 min plus 1 h chilling time

1 Heat the oven to 350°F (180°C / Gas Mark 4).
Line a 6-hole muffin pan with paper cases.

2 Sift the flour and baking powder into a mixing
bowl. Stir in the sugar and ground almonds.

3 Beat the eggs with the butter and milk. Stir in the
chopped almonds and orange zest.

4 Stir into the dry ingredients until just blended.
The mixture should be slightly lumpy.

5 Spoon into the paper cases, filling them three-
quarters full. Bake for 25–30 minutes until firm
and golden.

6 Cool in the tin for 5 minutes then place on a wire
rack to cool.

7 For the orange buttercream, beat the butter in a
bowl until light and creamy.

8 Gradually sift in the confectioners' (icing) sugar
with the orange juice and zest and beat well until
smooth. Chill for 1 hour.

9 Put the buttercream into a piping bag and pipe
on top of the muffins. Place a teaspoon of chopped
chocolate in the center of each muffin.

Makes 6 large muffins

CUPCAKES WITH ICE CREAM LAYERS

Ingredients

1 stick / 120 g butter

½ cup / 110 g superfine (caster) sugar

1 tsp vanilla extract

Heaped 1 cup / 120 g self-rising flour

Pinch of salt

1 tsp cornstarch (cornflour)

2 eggs, beaten

For the ice cream filling:

12 scoops strawberry ice cream

For the chocolate topping:

4 tbsp / 50 g butter

¼ cup / 20 g cocoa powder

½ cup / 75 g confectioners'
(icing) sugar

1 tsp vanilla extract

Method

Prep and cook time: 40 min

1 Heat the oven to 350°F (180°C / Gas Mark 4).
Place paper cases in a 12-hole bun tin.

2 Cream the butter and sugar until light and fluffy.
Stir in the vanilla.

3 Sift in the flour, salt and cornstarch (cornflour)
and lightly fold into the mixture alternately with the
eggs until well blended.

4 Spoon into the paper cases and bake for about
20–25 minutes until golden brown and springy to
the touch.

5 Allow to stand for 5 minutes, and then place on a
wire rack to cool.

6 Split each cupcake into three, using a sharp knife.
Place half a scoop of strawberry ice cream on one
layer and spread quickly over the cake. Top with a
layer of cupcake. Spread with another half scoop of
strawberry ice cream and top with the third layer of
cake. Place the cakes in the freezer.

7 For the chocolate topping, beat the butter until
soft and sift the cocoa powder over. Stir well, then
sift the confectioners' (icing) sugar over and add the
vanilla. Mix well.

8 Spread the topping over the top of each cake.
Place the cakes back in the freezer until you are
ready to serve.

Makes 12

CUPCAKES WITH ORANGE FILLING AND CHOCOLATE SAUCE

Ingredients

2 cups / 225 g self-rising flour

1 stick / 115 g butter

½ cup / 110 g sugar

Pinch of salt

1 egg beaten

Milk to mix

For the filling:

4 oz / 120 g packet orange gelatin (jelly)

1 tbsp orange marmalade

½ cup / 125 ml boiling water

To decorate:

6 oz / 175 g bittersweet (plain) chocolate (70% cocoa solids)

Method:

Prep and cook time: 40 min plus 2 hours chilling time

1 Heat the oven to 375°F (190°C / Gas Mark 5). Grease a 12-hole bun tin.

2 Sift the flour into a bowl and rub in the butter with your fingers until the mixture resembles fine breadcrumbs.

3 Stir in the sugar and salt, followed by the egg, and mix well. Add enough milk to give the mixture a soft dropping consistency.

4 Spoon the mixture into the bun tin and bake for 15–20 minutes until golden and firm. Leave in the tins for 3 minutes then place on a wire rack to cool.

5 For the filling, break up the gelatin (jelly) and put into a bowl with the marmalade and boiling water until the gelatin has dissolved. Stir and pour into a large dish or tin to form a ¼ inch (1cm) layer of gelatin. Leave to cool, and then chill until set.

6 When the gelatin (jelly) has set, cut out small rounds the same diameter as the cakes.

7 Split the cakes in half through the center using a sharp knife. Place a gelatin disk on top of one half and top with the other cake half.

8 Melt the chocolate in a bowl over a pan of simmering (not boiling) water.

9 Spoon chocolate over the cakes just before serving.

Makes 12

MINI MUFFINS
WITH ALMONDS

Ingredients

1 egg

¼ cup / 50 g sugar

Scant ½ cup / 110 ml milk

4 tbsp / 50 g butter, melted

A few drops of almond extract

1½ cups / 150 g all-purpose (plain) flour

½ tbsp baking powder

Pinch of salt

½ cup / 50 g flaked almonds

Confectioners' (icing) sugar for dusting

Method
Prep and cook time: 35 min

1 Heat the oven to 400ºF (200ºC / Gas Mark 6). Grease a 20-hole mini muffin pan.

2 Mix together the egg, sugar, milk, butter and almond extract in a mixing bowl until combined.

3 Sift in the flour, baking powder and salt and fold gently into the mixture until blended but still slightly lumpy.

4 Spoon the mixture into the muffin tins and place a few almonds on top of each muffin.

5 Bake for about 20 minutes until well risen. Allow to stand for 5 minutes then place on a wire rack to cool.

6 Sift a little confectioners' (icing) sugar over the muffins just before serving.

Makes 20

CHOCOLATE MUFFIN WITH CREAM FILLING

Ingredients

6 oz / 175 g bittersweet (plain) chocolate (70% cocoa solids), chopped

4 tbsp / 50 g butter

3 heaped cups / 375 g self-rising flour

1 tbsp baking powder

4 tbsp cocoa powder

½ cup / 100 g superfine (caster) sugar

1 egg

Scant 1½ cups / 350 ml milk

¾ cup / 75 g hazelnuts

1¼ cups / 300 ml whipping cream

Confectioners' (icing) sugar for dusting

Method

Prep and cook time: 45 min

1 Preheat the oven to 400°F (200°C / Gas Mark 6). Grease a 12-hole muffin pan.

2 Break the chocolate into a heatproof bowl and add the butter. Melt the chocolate and butter in a bowl standing over a saucepan of gently simmering water. Remove from the heat and stir once. Leave to cool slightly.

3 Sift the flour, baking powder and cocoa powder into a large bowl. Stir in the sugar.

4 Mix the egg and milk together and slowly stir into the melted chocolate. Stir the mixture into the dry ingredients until only just combined.

5 Spoon the mixture equally into the muffin cups and scatter a few hazelnuts over the top of each muffin.

6 Bake in the oven for 20–25 minutes until well risen and firm to the touch. Leave in the pan for 5 minutes and then place on a wire rack to cool.

7 Whisk the cream until stiff but not dry and spoon into a piping bag. When the muffins are cold, split them in half.

8 Pipe a swirl of cream on the bottom half of each muffin. Replace the tops and dust lightly with sifted confectioners' (icing) sugar.

Makes 12

REDCURRANT AND BLUEBERRY MUFFINS

Ingredients

2 eggs

4 tbsp / 50 g butter, melted

¾ cup / 175 ml milk

1 tsp vanilla extract

1¾ cups / 175 g all-purpose (plain) flour

¼ cup / 50 g sugar

2 tsp baking powder

1½ cups / 175 g mixed redcurrants and blueberries

For the topping:

1 cup / 120 g confectioners' (icing) sugar

1 tbsp hot water

Few drops of pink coloring

Method

Prep and cook time: 35 min

1 Heat the oven to 400°F (200°C / Gas Mark 6). Place paper cases in a 12-hole muffin pan.

2 Mix together the eggs, butter, milk and vanilla.

3 Sift the flour, sugar and baking powder into a mixing bowl and add the egg mixture. Stir gently with a fork until just combined. Fold in the redcurrants and blueberries.

4 Spoon into the paper cases and bake for 20–25 minutes until well risen and firm.

5 Leave to stand for 5 minutes then place on a wire rack to cool.

6 For the topping, sift the confectioners' (icing) sugar into a bowl and gradually beat in the hot water and a few drops of coloring. Drizzle over the cold muffins and leave to set.

Makes 12

BEE STING CUPCAKES

Ingredients

1 stick / 115 g butter, softened

Heaped ½ cup / 115 g superfine
(caster) sugar

1 egg, separated

7 tbsp honey plus ½ cup / 125 ml to
drizzle

2½ cups / 250 g all-purpose
(plain) flour

1 tsp baking soda (bicarbonate
of soda)

About 4 tbsp milk

1⅓ cups / 300 ml whipping cream

¾ cup / 75 g flaked almonds,
to decorate

Method

Prep and cook time: 45 min

1 Preheat the oven to 400°F (200°C / Gas Mark 6).
Grease an 18-hole muffin pan.

2 Put the butter and sugar in a large bowl and,
using an electric whisk, beat together until light
and fluffy. Beat in the egg yolk. Slowly add the 7
tablespoons of honey, beating well.

3 Sift in the flour and baking soda (bicarbonate
of soda) and gently stir into the mixture until just
combined. Add enough milk to give a soft dropping
consistency.

4 Whisk the egg white until stiff and then fold into
the mixture until incorporated. Spoon the mixture
equally into the muffin cups.

5 Bake in the oven for about 25 minutes until
golden and risen. Leave in the pan for 5 minutes and
then transfer to a wire rack and leave to cool.

6 Whisk the cream until stiff but not dry. Cut each
cupcake in half widthways and place a spoonful of
whipped cream on each flat half.

7 Drizzle with some of the remaining honey.
Replace the tops of the cupcakes and drizzle with
more honey. Press flaked almonds into the top of
each cupcake to decorate.

Makes 18

APRICOT AND GINGER MUFFINS

Ingredients

4 tbsp / 50 g butter, plus extra to grease the pan

1½ cups / 150 g all-purpose (plain) flour

½ tbsp baking powder

Pinch of salt

1 egg

¼ cup / 50 g superfine (caster) sugar

7 tbsp / 100 ml milk

1 tsp vanilla extract

¾ cup / 115 g chopped fresh apricots

For the topping:

5 tbsp / 75 g butter

2 tbsp corn (golden) syrup

1 cup / 125 g confectioners' (icing) sugar

½ cup / 75 g chopped candied (crystallized) ginger

Method

Prep and cook time: 45 min

1 Preheat the oven to 400°F (200°C / Gas Mark 6). Grease a 6-hole muffin pan.

2 Melt the butter. Sift the flour, baking powder and salt into a large bowl.

3 Mix together the egg, sugar, milk, vanilla extract and melted butter. Stir into the dry ingredients quickly until only just combined and still slightly lumpy.

4 Gently fold in the apricots. Spoon the mixture equally into the muffin cups.

5 Bake in the oven for 25–30 minutes until risen and golden brown.

6 Meanwhile, make the topping. Heat the butter, corn (golden) syrup and confectioners' (icing) sugar in a small saucepan over a medium heat for about 5 minutes until smooth. Stir in the ginger pieces.

7 Spoon on top of the partially cooked muffins for the last 5–8 minutes of the cooking time.

8 When the muffins are cooked and the topping is crisp, leave in the pan for 5 minutes and then transfer to a wire rack and leave to cool.

Makes 6

CHRISTMAS CUPCAKES

Ingredients

3 tsp / 20 g butter

2 eggs

½–⅔ cup / 120 g superfine (caster) sugar

3 tbsp whipping cream

½ cup / 115 g mincemeat

1 cup / 120 g self-rising flour

½ tsp baking powder

1 tsp ground cinnamon

½ tsp freshly grated nutmeg

2 tsp sherry

For the decoration:

4 oz / 120 g white marzipan

Red and green food colorings

Confectioners' (icing) sugar for dusting

Method

Prep and cook time: 35 min

1 Preheat the oven to 350°F (180°C / Gas Mark 4). Line a 12-hole muffin pan with paper cases.

2 Melt the butter. Mix the eggs and sugar together and beat in the cream. Gently stir in the mincemeat.

3 Sift in the flour, baking powder, cinnamon and nutmeg and fold in until incorporated.

4 Stir in the sherry and melted butter until well mixed. Spoon the mixture equally into the paper cases.

5 Bake in the oven for 12–15 minutes until risen and springy to the touch. Transfer to a wire rack and leave to cool.

6 Divide the marzipan in half. Knead a few drops of red coloring into one half and of green into the other half.

7 Roll out the marzipan on a surface lightly dusted with confectioners' (icing) sugar. Cut out festive shapes, such as stars and bells, with small cookie cutters.

8 Place the marzipan decorations on top of each cupcake and sift over a thick layer of confectioners' (icing) sugar to decorate.

Makes 12

APPLE MUFFINS WITH CARAMEL

Ingredients

2½ cups / 250 g all-purpose (plain) flour

1 heaped cup / 225 g superfine (caster) sugar

1 tbsp baking powder

1 tsp ground cinnamon

½ cup / 110 ml sunflower oil

2 eggs

¾ cup / 175 ml milk

1 apple, peeled and diced

For the caramel apple topping:

5 tbsp / 75 g butter

2 tbsp sugar

2 tbsp water

3 apples, peeled and thickly sliced

Method

Prep and cook time: 45 min

1 Heat the oven to 350ºF (180ºC / Gas Mark 4). Place paper cases in a 12-hole muffin pan.

2 Sift the flour, sugar, baking powder and cinnamon into a mixing bowl.

3 Mix together the oil, eggs and milk until combined. Stir into the dry ingredients until only just combined but still lumpy.

4 Gently fold in the apple.

5 Spoon into the paper cases and bake for 20–25 minutes until golden and risen.

6 Leave to stand for 2 minutes then place on a wire rack to cool.

7 For the topping, heat the butter, sugar and water in a pan until the sugar has dissolved. Bring to a boil. Add the apple slices and cook for 2–3 minutes, until soft and coated with syrup.

8 Invert the muffins onto a plate and spoon over the topping.

Makes 12

BUTTERFLY BUNS

Ingredients

2 eggs

1 cup / 110 g self-rising flour

½ teaspoon baking powder

1 stick / 110 g soft butter

½ cup / 110 g sugar

To decorate:

¾ cup / 175 g whipping cream

Confectioners' (icing) sugar

Method

Prep and cook time: 40 min

1 Heat the oven to 325ºF (170ºC / Gas Mark 3). Line a 12-hole muffin pan with paper cases.

2 Put all the ingredients for the cakes into a mixing bowl and whisk with an electric whisk until well combined. Alternatively, beat well with a wooden spoon.

3 Spoon the mixture into the paper cases and bake for about 30 minutes until the cakes are golden and springy to the touch.

4 Carefully cut round the tops of the cake with a cutter or sharp knife and remove the top of each cake. Slice the tops in half to form 2 "wings".

5 Whisk the cream until thick but not stiff. Spoon into a piping bag. Pipe a whirl onto each cake and press the "wings" into the cream. Sift over a little confectioners' (icing) sugar.

Makes 12

APPLE CAKES

Ingredients

2 eggs

½ cup / 110 g superfine (caster) sugar

1 cup / 110 g self-rising flour

1 stick / 110 g butter, melted

1 apple, peeled and diced

Confectioners' (icing) sugar,
to decorate

Method

Prep and cook time: 25 min

1 Heat the oven to 350°F (180°C / Gas 4). Grease a 12-hole bun tin.

2 Whisk the eggs and sugar together in a bowl until light and fluffy.

3 Gently fold in the flour and butter, followed by the apple.

4 Pour the mixture into the bun tin and bake for 8–10 minutes, until golden brown and a skewer inserted into one of the cakes comes out clean. Leave in the tins for 10 minutes, and then place on a wire rack to cool.

5 Sift over a little confectioners' (icing) sugar just before serving.

Makes 12

MINI CHERRY MUFFINS

Ingredients

5 tbsp / 75 g butter

⅓ cup / 75 g superfine (caster) sugar

2 eggs, beaten

¾ cup / 75 g self-rising flour

½ tsp almond extract

¾ cup / 110 g candied (glacé) cherries, chopped

For the frosting:

½ cup / 75 g confectioners' (icing) sugar

2 tsp hot water

To decorate:

24 whole fresh cherries

Method

Prep and cook time: 45 min

1 Heat the oven to 350°F (180°C / Gas Mark 4). Place paper cases in a 24-cup mini-muffin tin.

2 Beat the butter and sugar until light and fluffy. Gradually add the eggs, a little at a time, and beat well.

3 Sift in the flour and gently fold into the mixture with the almond extract and the cherries.

4 Spoon into the paper cases and bake for 12–15 minutes until golden and springy to the touch.

5 Place on a wire rack to cool.

6 For the frosting, sift the confectioners' (icing) sugar into a bowl and stir in enough hot water to make a thick frosting (icing).

7 Spread a little frosting on each cake and top with a fresh cherry.

Makes 24

CHOCOLATE MUFFINS WITH ORANGE CREAM

Ingredients

1½ sticks / 175 g butter

2 oz / 50g bittersweet (plain) chocolate (70% cocoa solids), chopped

1 cup / 120 g confectioners' (icing) sugar

¾ cup / 75 g all-purpose (plain) flour

1 tbsp cocoa powder

1 cup / 110 g ground almonds

1 tsp baking powder

Pinch of salt

6 egg whites

1 tsp vanilla extract

For the orange cream:

5 tbsp / 75 g butter

1¼ cups / 150 g confectioners' (icing) sugar

Juice of 1 orange

To decorate:

Grated zest

Method
Prep and cook time: 40 min

1 Heat the oven to 375°F (190°C / Gas Mark 5). Grease a 12-hole muffin pan.

2 Melt the butter and chocolate in a heatproof bowl over a pan of simmering (not boiling) water. Remove from the heat and stir gently to combine.

3 Sift the confectioners' (icing) sugar, flour and cocoa into a mixing bowl and stir in the almonds. Add the baking powder and salt.

4 Beat the egg whites lightly and stir into the dry ingredients with the vanilla.

5 Pour into the muffin pan and bake for about 20 minutes until risen and firm.

6 Leave to stand for 5 minutes, and then place on a wire rack to cool.

7 For the orange cream, whisk all the ingredients together in a small bowl until smooth and creamy.

8 Spoon a little orange cream on top of each muffin and decorate with grated orange zest.

Makes 12

BERRY CUPCAKES

Ingredients

1½ sticks / 175 g butter

1 tsp rosewater

1¼ cups / 125 g ground almonds

2 cups / 225 g confectioners'
(icing) sugar

9 tbsp all-purpose (plain) flour

6 egg whites

For the sauce:

Good ¾ cup / 200 ml water

1 cup / 200 g superfine (caster) sugar

14 oz / 400 g fresh or frozen mixed
summer berries

1 tsp rosewater

⅔ cup / 150 ml whipping cream,
to decorate

Method

Prep and cook time: 35 min

1 Preheat the oven to 375°F (190°C / Gas Mark 5).
Grease a 12-hole fluted muffin pan with butter or use
a silicone mold.

2 Melt the butter. Add the rosewater and mix together.

3 Put the ground almonds in a large bowl and sift in
the confectioners' (icing) sugar and flour.

4 Beat the egg whites lightly with a fork to combine
and then stir into the dry ingredients. Add the melted
butter mixture and mix gently until combined. Pour the
mixture equally into the prepared pan.

5 Bake in the oven for about 15 minutes until springy
to the touch. Leave in the pan for 2–3 minutes and then
transfer to a wire rack and leave to cool.

6 For the sauce, heat the water and sugar in a
saucepan over a low heat until the sugar has dissolved.
Add the mixed berries, bring to a boil and simmer for
5 minutes until the sauce has thickened. Stir in the
rosewater.

7 Pour a little of the sauce over and around each cake.

8 Whisk the cream until thick and spoon or pipe a
swirl on top of each cake to decorate before serving

Makes 12

FAIRY CAKES
WITH JAM FILLING

Ingredients

1 stick / 110 g butter

½ cup / 110 g superfine
(caster) sugar

2 eggs

1 cup / 110 g self-rising flour

1 teaspoon baking powder

½ cup / 75 g strawberry jelly (jam)

Method

Prep and cook time: 30 min

1 Heat the oven to 350°F (180°C / Gas Mark 4).
Line a 12-hole muffin pan with paper cases.

2 Put all the ingredients into a mixing bowl
and beat well for 2–3 minutes until the mixture is
well blended and smooth.

3 Spoon enough of the mixture into the muffin
cases to fill one-third full. Add a good teaspoon of
jam and cover with cake mixture.

4 Bake for 15–20 minutes until the cakes are risen
and golden. Cool the cakes on a wire rack.

Makes 12

ICED CHOCOLATE CUPCAKES

Ingredients

1 stick / 110 g butter (soft)

½ cup / 110 g sugar

2 eggs

1 cup / 110 g self-rising flour

1 teaspoon baking powder

1 tablespoon cocoa powder

For the frosting (icing):

4 tbsp / 50 g butter

Scant 1 cup / 110 g confectioners'
(icing) sugar

½ teaspoon vanilla extract

2 tablespoons whipping cream

To decorate:

2 oz / 50 g grated chocolate

Method

Prep and cook time: 30 min

1 Heat the oven to 325°F (170°C / Gas Mark 3).
Line a 12-hole muffin pan with paper muffin cases.

2 Put all the cupcake ingredients into a mixing
bowl and beat well with an electric whisk or
wooden spoon until well mixed.

3 Spoon into the paper cases and bake for about
20 minutes until risen and firm. Cool on a wire rack.

4 For the frosting (icing), beat the butter until soft
and sift in the confectioners' (icing) sugar.

5 Add the vanilla and beat well. Beat in just enough
cream to form a frosting with a creamy consistency.
Spread thickly on top of the cakes.

6 Sprinkle with grated chocolate to finish.

Makes 12

RASPBERRY AND COCONUT MUFFINS

Ingredients

2¼ cups / 225 g all-purpose (plain) flour

1 tbsp baking powder

Heaped ½ cup / 110 g sugar

2 eggs

1 stick / 120 g butter, melted

¾ cup / 175 ml milk

2 cups / 175 g sweetened shredded coconut

1 cup / 110 g fresh raspberries

Confectioners' (icing) sugar for dusting

Method

Prep and cook time: 35 min

1 Heat the oven to 350°F (180°C / Gas Mark 4). Grease a 12-hole muffin pan.

2 Sift the flour and baking powder into a mixing bowl and stir in the sugar.

3 Mix together the eggs, butter and milk until combined. Stir into the dry ingredients until only just mixed and still slightly lumpy.

4 Gently stir in the coconut and raspberries. Spoon the mixture into the muffin pan, filling each hole three-quarters full.

5 Bake for 20–25 minutes until golden and risen.

6 Leave in to stand for 3 minutes, and then place on a wire rack to cool.

7 Sift confectioners' (icing) sugar over the muffins just before serving.

Makes 12

CHOCOLATE MUFFINS WITH FONDANT FILLING

Ingredients

2 sticks plus 2 tbsp /250 g butter

Cocoa powder to dust the pan

7 oz / 200 g bittersweet (plain) chocolate (70% cocoa solids), chopped

4 eggs plus 4 egg yolks

1 cup / 200 g superfine (caster) sugar

2 cups / 200 g all-purpose (plain) flour

To decorate:

Fresh cherries

Method

Prep and cook time: 35 min plus 30 min chilling time

1 Melt 3 ½ tablespoons of the butter and use to grease a 9-hole muffin pan. Dust each muffin cup with cocoa powder to completely coat the butter.

2 Break the chocolate into a heatproof bowl and add the remaining butter. Melt the chocolate and butter in a bowl standing over a saucepan of gently simmering water. Remove from the heat and stir until smooth. Leave to cool slightly.

3 Put the eggs, egg yolks and sugar in a large bowl and whisk together using an electric whisk until thick and pale.

4 Sift the flour into the eggs and then beat together.

5 Gradually beat the melted chocolate into the egg mixture until the mixture is completely combined.

6 Spoon the mixture equally into the muffin cups. Chill in the refrigerator for at least 30 minutes.

7 Preheat the oven to 400°F (200°C / Gas Mark 6). Bake the muffins in the oven for 12–15 minutes until the tops have formed a crust and the muffins are starting to come away from the sides of their molds. Leave in the pan for 2 minutes before removing them gently.

8 Serve warm, decorated with a fresh cherry on top.

Makes 9

RASPBERRY MUFFINS WITH VANILLA CREAM

Ingredients

For the muffins:

1¾ cups / 200 g self-rising flour

2 tsp baking powder

1 stick plus 6 tbsp / 200 g butter, softened

4 eggs

1 cup / 200 g superfine (caster) sugar

3 tbsp milk

½ cup / 50 g ground almonds

5 oz / 150 g fresh raspberries

For the vanilla cream:

1⅓ cups / 300 ml whipping cream

2 tbsp confectioners' (icing) sugar

Few drops of vanilla extract

Fresh raspberries, to decorate

Method

Prep and cook time: 45 min

1 Heat the oven to 350°F (180°C / Gas Mark 4). Place paper cases in a 12-hole muffin pan.

2 Put all the muffin ingredients except the raspberries into a mixing bowl and whisk with an electric whisk until smooth. Alternatively beat well with a wooden spoon.

3 Gently stir in the raspberries.

4 Spoon the mixture into the paper cases to half fill them and bake for 20–25 minutes until golden and risen.

5 Leave to stand for 5 minutes and then place on a wire rack to cool.

6 For the vanilla cream, whisk the cream until stiff but not dry. Sift in the confectioners' sugar and stir into the cream with the vanilla.

7 Put the cream into a piping bag and pipe onto each muffin. Top with fresh raspberries.

HAZELNUT AND CHOCOLATE CUPCAKES

Ingredients

6 oz / 175 g 70% cocoa solids dark chocolate

4 tbsp / 50 g butter

3½ cups / 375 g self-rising flour

1 tbsp baking powder

4 tbsp cocoa powder

½ cup / 100 g sugar

1 large egg

1½ cups / 350 ml milk

2½ oz / 75 g ground hazelnuts

For the filling:

1¼ cups / 300 ml whipping cream

To decorate:

Confectioners' (icing) sugar

Method

Prep and cook time: 45 min

1 Heat the oven to 400°F (200°C / Gas Mark 6). Grease a 12-hole muffin tin.

2 Melt the chocolate and butter in a heatproof bowl over a pan of simmering (not boiling) water. Remove from the heat and stir once.

3 Sift the flour, baking powder and cocoa powder into a mixing bowl. Stir in the sugar.

4 Mix the egg and milk together and slowly stir into the melted chocolate. Stir the mixture into the dry ingredients until only just combined.

5 Spoon into the muffin cups and scatter a few hazelnuts over the top of each muffin.

6 Bake for 20-25 minutes until well risen and firm. Cool in the tins for 5 minutes then place on a wire rack to cool.

7 When the muffins are cold, split them in half.

8 Whisk the cream until stiff but not dry and spoon into a piping bag.

9 Pipe a swirl of cream on each muffin half. Replace the tops and dust lightly with confectioners' (icing) sugar.

Makes 12

BLACKBERRY AND RASPBERRY MUFFINS

Ingredients

1¾ cups / 175 g all-purpose (plain) flour

2 teaspoons baking powder

½ cup / 110 g sugar

1 stick / 110 g butter, melted

1 egg

½ cup / 120 ml milk

½ cup / 110 g blackberries

½ cup / 110 g raspberries

For the topping:

2 oz / 50 g finely chopped almonds

¼ cup / 50 g sugar

3 tbsp flour

3 tbsp / 45 g butter, melted

Method

Prep and cook time: 35 min

1 Heat the oven to 350ºF (180ºC / Gas Mark 4). Grease a 12 cup muffin tin.

2 Sift the flour and baking powder into a mixing bowl and stir in the sugar.

3 Beat the melted butter with the egg and milk and gradually stir into the dry ingredients until just mixed but still slightly lumpy.

4 Gently stir in the blackberries and raspberries.

5 Spoon into the muffin cups, filling almost to the top.

6 For the topping, mix all the ingredients together and spoon a little over the top of each muffin.

7 Bake for about 25 minutes until risen and firm.

8 Leave to stand for 5 minutes, then place on a wire rack to cool.

Makes 12

HUMMINGBIRD CAKES

Ingredients

3¾ cups / 375 g self-rising flour

1 tsp ground cinnamon

Heaped 1 cup / 225 g superfine
(caster) sugar

2 ripe bananas

2 eggs, beaten

½ cup / 100 ml sunflower oil

5 oz / 150 g chopped pecans

16 oz / 440 g can crushed pineapple,
drained

For the lemon cream:

1 stick / 115 g butter, softened

3 cups / 375 g confectioners'
(icing) sugar

2 tbsp whipping cream

2 tsp lemon juice

¼ tsp vanilla extract

6 tbsp chopped toasted pecans,
to decorate

Method

Prep and cook time: 50 min

1 Preheat the oven to 350°F (180°C / Gas Mark 4). Grease a 12-hole muffin pan.

2 Sift the flour and cinnamon into a large bowl. Stir in the sugar.

3 Put the bananas in a bowl and mash well with a fork.

4 Add the bananas to the dry ingredients with the egg, oil, pecans and pineapple. Stir until the mixture is just combined, but still slightly lumpy. Divide the mixture equally into the muffin cups.

5 Bake in the oven for 30–35 minutes, until golden brown and risen. Leave in the pan for 5 minutes and then transfer to a wire rack and leave to cool.

6 To make the lemon cream, put the butter in a large bowl and beat with an electric whisk until creamy. Gradually beat in the confectioners' (icing) sugar, then beat in the cream, lemon juice and vanilla extract. Beat well until light and fluffy.

7 Invert the muffins and spread with the lemon cream. Decorate with some chopped toasted pecan nuts.

Makes 12

GINGERBREAD BUNS

Ingredients

1 stick / 115 g butter

2½ cups / 250 g all-purpose (plain) flour

1 heaped cup / 225 g superfine (caster) sugar

2 tsp baking powder

2 tsp ground ginger

½ tsp ground cinnamon

2 eggs

3 tbsp honey

3 tbsp ginger syrup and 2 tbsp chopped preserved ginger

¾ cup / 175 ml hot water

Confectioners' (icing) sugar, to decorate

Method

Prep and cook time: 40 min

1 Preheat the oven to 350°F (180°C / Gas Mark 4). Grease a 12-hole muffin pan.

2 Melt the butter. Sift the flour, sugar, baking powder, ginger and cinnamon into a large bowl.

3 Beat together the eggs, honey, ginger syrup and butter until smooth. Stir into the dry ingredients.

4 Add the water and chopped ginger and stir well until combined. Spoon the mixture equally into the muffin cups.

5 Bake in the oven for 20–25 minutes until golden brown and a skewer inserted into the center comes out clean. Leave in the pan for 10 minutes and then transfer to a wire rack and leave to cool.

6 Sift a little confectioners' (icing) sugar over the buns to decorate just before serving.

Makes 12

ANGELFOOD CUPCAKES

Ingredients

1 cup / 110 g all-purpose (plain) flour

1/3 cup / 50 g confectioners' (icing) sugar

10 large egg whites

1/2 tsp salt

1 tsp vanilla extract

1 tsp cream of tartar

Generous 3/4 cup / 175 g sugar

For the vanilla cream:

6 tbsp water

1 3/4 cups / 350 g superfine (caster) sugar

6 egg whites

3 sticks / 350 g butter

1 tsp vanilla extract

To decorate:

Chopped candied (crystallized) ginger

Method

Prep and cook time: 1 hour

1 Heat the oven to 325ºF (170ºC / Gas Mark 3). Place paper cases in an 18-hole bun tin.

2 Mix the flour with the confectioners' (icing) sugar.

3 Whisk the egg whites with the salt, vanilla and cream of tartar in a large bowl until softly peaking. Gradually whisk in the sugar, 1 tablespoon at a time, until the whites are firm and glossy.

4 Sift the flour mixture over the egg whites, folding gently until everything is well combined. Spoon the mixture into the paper cases.

5 Bake for 12–15 minutes until the cupcakes are springy and golden. Place the cupcakes on a wire rack to cool.

6 For the vanilla cream, heat the water and sugar in a pan over a low heat until the sugar is dissolved. Bring to a boil and boil for 3-4 minutes until the mixture is syrupy. Remove from the heat.

7 Whisk the egg whites in a large bowl until softly peaking. Gradually pour on the syrup in a steady stream, whisking constantly for 10-15 minutes until the mixture is thick and cold.

8 Beat the butter until soft and creamy. Gradually add the egg white mixture with the vanilla, whisking well, until the mixture is thick and smooth.

9 Spoon the vanilla cream on top of each cake, swirling with a knife. Scatter with candied ginger.

Makes 18

CHOCOLATE AND BANANA MUFFINS

Ingredients

1 cup / 120 g self-rising flour

2/3 cup / 120 g sugar

1 tsp baking soda (bicarbonate of soda)

Pinch of salt

½ tsp ground cinnamon

3½ oz / 100 g bittersweet (plain) chocolate (70% cocoa solids), chopped

1 egg, beaten

1 stick / 120 g butter, melted

1 tsp vanilla extract

2 very ripe bananas

For the topping:

6 banana slices

Melted butter

Method

Prep and cook time: 45 min

1 Heat the oven to 350ºF (180ºC / Gas 4). Grease a 6-hole muffin tin.

2 Sift the flour, sugar, baking soda (bicarbonate of soda) salt and cinnamon into a mixing bowl. Stir in the chopped chocolate.

3 Make a well in the center and add the beaten egg, warm butter and vanilla.

4 Mash the bananas well and stir into the mixture until just combined, but still slightly lumpy.

5 Spoon the mixture into the holes of the muffin tin and top each with a slice of banana. Brush the banana slices with a little melted butter.

6 Bake for 25–30 minutes until firm and risen. Leave in the tin for 5 minutes, then place on a wire rack to cool.

Makes 6

CINNAMON AND MACADAMIA MUFFINS

Ingredients

4 tbsp / 50 g butter

¾ cup / 175 ml milk

2 eggs, beaten

2¼ cups / 225 g all-purpose (plain) flour

4 tsp baking powder

1 tsp ground cinnamon

Pinch of salt

Heaped ½ cup / 115 g light brown sugar

½ cup / 75 g coarsely chopped toasted macadamia nuts

For the topping:

6 tbsp coarse sugar crystals or sugar

½ cup / 75 g coarsely chopped toasted macadamia nuts

Method

Prep and cook time: 30 min

1 Preheat the oven to 400°F (200°C/Gas Mark 6). Grease a 12-hole muffin pan.

2 Melt the butter and leave to cool. Add the milk and eggs and mix together.

3 Sift the flour, baking powder, cinnamon and salt into a large bowl. Stir in the sugar and the macadamia nuts.

4 Pour the egg mixture into the dry ingredients and stir until only just combined and the mixture is still slightly lumpy.

5 Spoon the mixture equally into the muffin cups. Sprinkle with the coarse sugar and macadamia nuts.

6 Bake in the oven for 15–18 minutes until risen and golden brown. Leave in the pan for 5 minutes and then transfer to a wire rack and leave to cool.

Makes 12

CARROT MUFFINS WITH WALNUTS

Ingredients

Heaped 1 cup / 225 g sugar

3 eggs

1 cup / 200 ml sunflower oil

2 cups / 225 g whole-wheat (wholemeal) flour

1 tsp ground cinnamon

Pinch of salt

12 oz / 350 g grated carrots

1 cup / 175 g walnuts chopped

For the topping:

1 cup / 225 g cream cheese

2 tbsp light brown sugar

1 tbsp orange juice

Cinnamon

Method

Prep and cook time: 40 min plus 30 min chilling time

1 Heat the oven to 350°F (180°C / Gas Mark 4). Place paper cases in a 10-hole bun tin.

2 Beat together the sugar, eggs and oil until light and frothy.

3 Stir in the flour, cinnamon and salt and beat until combined. Stir in the carrots and walnuts.

4 Spoon into the paper cases and bake for 20–25 minutes until firm and risen. Place on a wire rack to cool.

5 For the topping, beat the ingredients together until smooth. Chill for 30 minutes.

6 Spread the topping over the top of the cakes and dust with a little cinnamon.

Makes 10

LEMON CUPCAKES

Ingredients

1 stick / 115 g butter, softened

Heaped ½ cup / 115 g superfine (caster) sugar

Finely grated zest of 2 lemons plus 2 tbsp juice

2 eggs, beaten

⅓ cup / 75 ml milk

1½ cups / 150 g all-purpose (plain) flour

1 tsp baking powder

Pinch of salt

Heaped 1 cup / 150 g confectioners' (icing) sugar

Method

Prep and cook time: 40 min

1 Preheat the oven to 375°F (190°C / Gas Mark 5). Line a 12-hole muffin pan with paper muffin cases.

2 Put the butter and sugar in a large bowl and, using an electric whisk, beat together until light and fluffy.

3 Beat in the half the lemon zest, the eggs and milk, a little at a time, until combined.

4 Sift in the flour, baking powder and salt and gently fold into the mixture until well mixed. Spoon the mixture equally into the muffin cases.

5 Bake in the oven for about 20 minutes until golden brown and springy to the touch. Leave in the pan for 5 minutes and then transfer to a wire rack and leave to cool.

6 To make the frosting, sift the confectioners' (icing) sugar into a bowl and stir in the lemon juice, mixing well until smooth.

7 Spoon a teaspoon of frosting on top of each cupcake, spreading it out to cover the tops completely. Sprinkle a little of the remaining lemon zest on top of each cupcake to decorate.

Makes 12

CHOCOLATE CHIP MUFFINS

Ingredients

1 stick / 110 g butter

1/3 cup / 75 g white sugar

2 tbsp light brown sugar

2 eggs beaten

1¾ cups / 175 g all-purpose (plain) flour

1 tbsp baking powder

7 tbsp / 110 ml milk

½ tbsp vanilla extract

1 cup / 175 g chocolate chips

To decorate:

Confectioners' (icing) sugar

Method

Prep and cook time: 35 min

1 Heat the oven to 375°F (190°C / Gas Mark 5). Place paper cases in a 12 hole muffin tin.

2 Beat the butter and both sugars until light and fluffy.

3 Beat in the eggs, a little at a time, mixing well.

4 Sift the flour and baking powder into the mixture and fold in gently with the milk and vanilla.

5 Gently stir in half the chocolate chips.

6 Spoon the mixture into the paper cases. Sprinkle the remaining chocolate chips over the top of each muffin.

7 Bake for 20–25 minutes until golden and risen. Leave in the tins for 5 minutes, then place on a wire rack to cool.

8 Sift a little confectioners' (icing) sugar over the muffins just before serving.

Makes 12

Published by Transatlantic Press

First published in 2011

Transatlantic Press
38 Copthorne Road, Croxley Green, Hertfordshire WD3 4AQ

© Transatlantic Press

Images and Recipes by StockFood © The Food Image Agency

Recipes selected by Jonnie Léger, StockFood

A catalogue record for this book is available from the British Library.

ISBN 978-1-907176-44-9

Printed in China